Anthony always asks for apples.

Bertha

plays banjo while eating a bagel.

Crazy Chris chases coconuts!

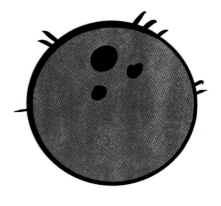

Dexter

Dunkin digs while eating doughnuts.

Eager Edna eats Edgar's eggplants.

Frankie
finds fun
in flinging
fruit.

Gloria

grows
gigantic
grapes.

Happy Hugo has humongous hands!

Ilene is ignoring her indigo iguana.

Janice
jumps jars of jam while listening to jazz.

King Kevin kindly kicks kickballs.

Lewis
loves licking lollipops loudly.

Marvelous Mandy makes mulberry milkshakes.

Nutty Nick wears noodles on his noggin.

Olivia Owl

only eats organic oranges.

Patrick's purple pig prefers pop corn.

Queen Quinn likes quality quinces.

Rick runs 'round red rocks.

Susan's socks smell so stinky!

Timmy Tommy tasted ten tomatoes today.

Ulysses' underwear is under a used umbrella.

Viking Victoria is very vocal about vegetables!

Wendle wants warm water. What a weirdo!

Xavier

plays a xylophone while getting an X-ray.

Yolanda
yelled
YIPPEE!
at yoga
yesterday.

Zany Zobel zips, zaps, and zoooooms!

David Zobel - Designer/Illustrator

dzobel.com | 443.691.3914
david@dzobel.com

Made in the USA
Lexington, KY
07 October 2017